Another Creature

Another Creature

POEMS BY
PAMELA GEMIN

The University of Arkansas Press
Fayetteville
2010

ISBN-10: 1-55728-928-X
ISBN-13: 978-1-55728-928-5

14   13   12   11   10   5   4   3   2   1

Text design by Ellen Beeler

♾ The paper used in this publication meets the minimum
requirements of the American National Standard for Permanence
of Paper for Printed Library Materials Z39.48-1984.

Library of Congress Cataloging-in-Publication Data

Gemin, Pamela, 1954–
    Another creature : poems / by Pamela Gemin.
    p. cm.
    ISBN 978-1-55728-928-5 (pbk. : alk. paper)
    PS3557.E424 A8 2010
    811'.54—dc22

                                                        2009047709

In memory of Eugene Haun, 1920–2006

. . . day after day, the rumbling
of a platform in the past
where I am sixteen
and waiting for a train
while down the street
an old, deaf woman
is planting cabbage behind a shed.
  —Laura Kasischke, "Cyclone"

Let my questions stand unsolved
Like trees around a pond. Water's cold lick
Is a response. I swim across the ring of it.
  —Alicia Ostriker, "Middle-Aged Woman at a Pond"

Acknowledgments

Thanks to the following journals in which these poems first appeared, sometimes under different titles: *Blaze*, "And Woke Up Vanishing," "My Brother Calls Me from His Boat," "Tiger"; *Chattahoochee Review*, "Destiny Car," "Panic in Detroit"; *Cimarron Review*, "Dean Walters' Dream," "Lucinda's Voice," "My Neighbor's Fence," "This Is Not My Beautiful House"; *Crania*, "Felonious"; *Del Sol Review*, "Junction," "Lawns," "My Father's Drums"; *Eclectica*, "Covet," "Drinking Man," "I Remember How This Song Goes," "That Teenage Feeling"; *Green Mountains Review*, "At Ragdale," "Leaf by Leaf," "Minnesota," "Newlywed"; *Margie*, "A Particular Shadow," "A Smoke," "Blue Lake Fantasy #4"; *Perihelion*, "The Goat"; *Primavera*, "Sweet Engine"; *Puerto del Sol*, "Another Creature," "The Man Who Says Pain Is a Friend"; *Prairie Schooner*, "Oh Honey"; *Rattle*, "Ravenous," "Girls and Lakes," "Sparks"; *Rhino*, "Fat Woman with Fishburger, Fries"; *Southern Poetry Review*, "Faculty Wife with Hummus," "Morning Swim"; *Spoon River Poetry Review*, "Room-Darkening Shades," "Still Enough"; *Valparaiso Poetry Review*, "Bottom of the Cup," "Desire," "Raspberries," "What's Going On."

Thanks to *Poetry Daily* for reprinting "Dean Walters' Dream."

Thanks to those whose attention to these poems has made all the difference: Robert Alexander, David Graham, Joan Houlihan, Josie Kearns, Tania Rochelle, Paula Sergi, Betsy Sholl, Kate Sontag, Victoria Redel, Ron Rindo, Erin Tapley, Leslie Ullman, Gale Walden, and David Wojahn.

I am grateful as well to the Wisconsin Arts Board for the fellowship that enabled this work and to the Ragdale Foundation for its generous gifts of time and space.

Thanks to my parents, William and Patricia Pierce, and to my husband Joseph Gemin, as well as all whose friendship and encouragement have sustained my writing these many years, especially Becky

Fitzhenry, Marguerite Helmers, Paul Klemp, Julie MacRury, Janet Norton, Rich Rummel, Sue Rummel, Ellen Shriner, and Alison Townsend.

To Julie King, first reader, fine writer, and cherished friend, my gratitude forever.

And finally, to Enid Shomer, series editor, my deepest respect and thanks.

Contents

I

Sweet Engine

God for the furnace, god for the fire, god
for the engine of love, where are you now?
I'd have offered my willing throat to your soldier,

crumpled beneath his cloak's red hem.
Instead I climbed the rickety ladder welded
to the side of my apartment house, thirty

feet up to a black tar roof to lay myself oiled
and shining in June sun, a burning offering.
Cigarettes, radio, sunscreen rolled in a fish-print

towel around my neck, little red Igloo made
for a six pack in my left hand. The ladder's black
enamel held bright heat. Sometimes a sandal

would slip and I'd stop to toss it above my head,
where it stuck in the sandy tar. Sometimes
the towel cape unfurled and scattered its goods

below in the weedy alley. Is it now I should say
one has to be drunk to make a climb like this,
and young enough? Thirty feet up to drink beer

and smoke and burn down the afternoon waiting,
while under their rooftop ceiling the ancient
Johannsen sisters watched their game shows

and softly applauded, rocking in heirloom chairs
and drinking weak lemonade; and under their rockers'
rungs, their braided rugs and slippered feet, my own

kitchen sat with its huge white stove waiting, cold
dishes waiting in the old chipped porcelain sink,
greasy shades drawn down tight and a ticking clock

and a telephone not ringing. But then around three
your blue pickup sighted: two blocks north, chugging
its way up Pine to my very street! Your blue truck

downshifting one block to my building, downshifting
again and making its turn, sweet engine, into my parking
lot. And then its door slamming, steps up the porch

and your feathery knock, my belly-down inching,
girl soldier, out to the edge of roof, the top of your blessed
head turning as you rang the bell. I might have rained

my venom down upon you. I might have bounced
a beer can off your head. But I couldn't stop watching,
you running a hand through to smooth thick hair, you

stepping around to the window to rap on glass.
Couldn't stop watching my self-not-there, the woman
you wanted after all, away for the afternoon.

Lawns

All over my city, on streets named for trees
    and presidents, lawns have come back, dotted
        with violets and tulip cups.

Days when one foot would not
    follow the other, days when the dishes
        lay cool in the sink, days

when I knew I'd die, I wanted
    to stretch face down on lawns like these, the taste
        of green blades in my mouth, stained

ankles twisting. A Saturday father might
    find a soft bump in the leaves beneath his rake tines.
        Mealy bone he sprinkled to the lilies might be mine.

Days when I knew the widths and lengths
    of every stray feather, every dead yardbird's claw,
        the full perimeter of fear, would he have sniffed

the air and fenced me out? Or cranked on the sprinklers
    and wrapped a sweet twine of myrtle around my throat,
        then let the fat robins rain down.

Dean Walters' Dream

And after you'd sobered up, did you find yourself
bootless, barefoot, lost on your walk
through our neighborhood park, trying to find East
by the sun's diagram, first frost of October
under your calloused toes? And scared
shitless—where was your leather jacket, the one
you bought in Vegas for a song, broken so far
into butter a woman could pour her face
into your collar? And where were
your favorite cap, your lucky darts?
When the headache crowned, did you recall
the gentle slope of our still-green lawn, the ash leaves
curled to crisps of gold around your face?
Were you thinking you'd rest
five minutes before you knocked again,
kicked in the flimsy screen to pound
on the inside door—is that when you surrendered,
pulled off your boots and socks, rolled the soft leather
under your head and floated into strange language:
where is my leafy smoke,
red flannel moon, and oh where
have you flung me this time?
When we awoke the officers came
and shook their heads at your empty boots
and jacket, examined the crumpled
check in your pocket signed Dean H. Walters.

Drunk must have thought he lived here, they surmised.
But as you bled your dreams into our grass,
we dreamt above you, twin clouds of enemy soldiers
and old boyfriends tethered by dream bubbles
to our slumbering heads.
Halt you are under arrest produce your papers
I love you more than Colt 45
    And deep as you slept, we slept too,
through your banging and howling, our sound machine
churning out ocean-electric waves across fitful snoring,
through gutturals slamming the stairwell shut
and hammering staccato heels. Through Benny Wyzinski
kissing and kissing my neck on the vinyl recliner.
Where is my leafy smoke, red flannel moon, and oh where am I?

Destiny Car

Some nights we meet out on the killer highway
one girl was scooped off of, paralyzed for life.
Another died head-on with a family of four
while her girlfriends danced on, in the glittering
wreck of The Dome, and we whispered
I love you   No I love you more

Here in Dreamland we're made of lips
and tongues. Here we are ageless, disembodied,
pure smoke of intuition, goofy-stoned. My tiny
dream hands in the hollows of your dream
shoulders. Over the MC5's thwack and clobber,
Earth life calls *come back, come back*, the way

the still-living call out to the gone. Come back
to the tangled garden, the stink of petunias,
the driveway cracks. The cupboards full of rain
and cereal bowls. But here we are seventeen
and your slim boy hips, your hair loose
from its ponytail, the electric plea

let me be who I am
in the sound
that abounds
and resounds
and rebounds
off the ceiling

And what does it mean when The Dome
catches fire, the way our parents always
knew it would, hot grease and battered
onions? When we lose each other in the crush
of teens pushing toward one exit, I find
my green velvet jacket, my favorite scarf

in the parking lot, soaked with your Brut
cologne. *Climb into the destiny car,*
someone says, and I'm driving the killer
highway alone, back home to my fenced-in
yard and my steady man, onion
patchouli smoke clinging to my hair.

Another Creature

Because I was seventeen, eighteen, drunk
beyond pain or surprise, I said
go ahead and show me.
Drive-in sky, car windows cranked down,
swell of fresh bites rising pink on bare
patches of belly and thigh.
Violet dusk and darkening line of poplars
past the screen, film slipping off
its reel in long white stripes, the whine
of warplanes lost to honking horns.
Here's how you make me feel, you said,
and lowered your Marlboro just beyond
the narrowing of wrist, the white snake's
throat. And brought it down slowly
to give me a chance to flinch,
but I did not flinch. You said you loved me
as much as your mother, your spaniel,
your new Camaro, and proof of it bubbled
up clear on my skin, circle of bleached white
moon crater ridged where burning ash
met flesh and made this scar, here,
when you were a boy and I was another creature.

Sparks

Charlie claims that's where his momma made him,
so what he remembers best is the fragrance of backseat
leather, the pillows and creases that stick to the backs
of bare legs. Charlie has borrowed the Rolls tonight,
some old Miami fart's pride and joy sent in for detail
striping. By day you're the ponytailed girl who shines
cars for Charlie, out back in your green bikini top
and cutoffs. Down here on the beach it's as easy to hire
cute as ugly, Charlie says, so he hires cute. By night
you're the glamour girl with the Zsa Zsa updo,
thrift store rhinestones in your twist, another gift
from Charlie. He borrows the fanciest cars to take you
dancing on the strip, for surf and turf at the famous
revolving restaurant at the pier. Sometimes you get so drunk
on Singapore Slings that you lose your way back
from the ladies' room, a girl stumbling out of a toilet stall,
into a spinning world on slingback pumps. Sometimes
the steak's too pink for you, sometimes hot butter drips
off the chunks of lobster you hold aloft with your tiny fork,
trying to catch a stray thought or articulate a point. *My daughter
don't hold her liquor so well,* he explains to frowning waiters.
Charlie Sparks says, with him, a girl never has to do anything
she doesn't want, though it might feel nice and it wouldn't hurt.
He'd never turn down a sweet goodnight kiss, for instance.
But Charlie's a patient man. He likes the wait.

Girls and Lakes

When girls are small, their fathers toss them
   off boats and watch as they sink and surface
      flapping, little bird-fish that they are,
         mouthspouts raised to suck air.

Whatever animal fear they know is roughly
   licked away, by waves or air currents
      or songs of gulls crossing sky. On the dock
         girls sing and comb each other's hair,

catch Jesus spiders, let them go.
   Later their boyfriends frown as they pinch
      the soft woman-dough their bikinis cut into,
         succulent pillowing swells at their breast tops

and thighs, satiny spills of hips not danced
   or kicked or starved away. And when they are full
      grown creatures they unwrap the towels
         from their waists and let them fall, or gingerly

slip off their t-shirts behind the pine rows.
   Walking with pride or shame through broken shells
      to the sand that takes their footprints, they adjust
         sagging straps, suck in a good lunch. But the moment

their ankles cut the first ripples, all of their body's water
    remembers: wading into lakes they know their legs'
        awful strength, shiver off waves that rise to their kneecaps,
            crotches, shoulders, the tips of their hair,

and know themselves buoyant, invincible,
    offering their lovely heads unto the lakes,
        and weightless—the way they have always
            wanted to feel, entirely received.

Fat Woman with Fishburger, Fries

So long chopping carrots and counting
grams, she's almost forgotten
that taste on her tongue of fryer and salt
and sauce as she crosses herself and clutches
the bun with both hands and sighs, *my fault,*
my most grievous fault, bright yen
beyond hunger dancing down her body's hot
rungs, a signal in neon like molten
light taking its horrible form in a knot
of want, want, all of what's in this sack
to its greasy bottom. Forget the pink
bras of sixteen, fold the honeymoon back
to the apple and its ideal; just *think*
this desire away: *Who was the girl with snail shell*
nipples, soaping her breasts with rose
and lavender foam? Look under the swell
of her raised arm: a spray of tiny moles.
And below: a delicate belly dent, live oyster
of sex open-hinged. Was she ever that creature,
copper hair spread full across a grateful lover's
chest? Did she ever imagine the future
of her body's cravings, lust estranged,
warped into this wondrous shape, sweet
riddles of hunger and flesh exchanged,
robust, resplendent, plentiful, replete?

My Neighbor's Fence

In their loosening, tightening V, the southbound geese flap
and bark their goodbyes to the wacky makeshift fence
she's erected the month since my neighbor's stopped speaking to me
(*You're not even listening, are you, to my stories?*),
the month since her marriage crumbled like bone-dry leaves
that blow over from our shedding maple, a fence to keep us
and our foliage OUT—NO TRESPASS—OUT!!! of the sweep of her rage.

Nine summer screens, the cage of a grown child's rabbit long
buried under bulbs' rusty sleep and grubs' tight coilings.
Three upside down trash cans, stack-n-store lawn chairs cracked
with the weight of tipsy relations eating from soggy plates
in her back yard. A friendly mutant zoo in molded plastic.
And Pick 'n Save bags, brimming with brittle sticks.

She must really hate you bad, says my teenage son. *If you want
I'll go over and moon her,* he offers, so kindly I almost take him up—
a full autumn moon shining over my neighbor's crazy fence,
the full kind of crazy she's finally gone, the forty-some moons
she's collected this rubble, cobbled together to stand, goddamn it,
for something, *something* to show for the diapers, the car pools,
the bottom-burned cookies, the casserole scraps afloat in cold
dishwater. She's leaving the floodlights on and hooking the screens.
She's covering mirrors with black satin, chiffon, and lace from her trousseau
(*I don't think you've ever heard a word I've said*).

And Lord in my own list of days you have seen me thus.
Howling full-blown mad in moonlight, demented or drunk
enough to raise a fence from whatever trash is left me, mean
streaks aflame in my hair. And Lord spare my boy
the world's broken pudding skin, spoon cutting
into the soft sweet places we hide when the edges peel back
and the borders fall away. May your lightning not strike
my neighbor's blue plastic schnauzer, sitting mute watch
with lizard and hen. Nor her red-hatted gnome
with its pointy ears, grinning its horrible grin.

Trash Night

Dare you to tell a possum cravings pass.
Dare you to tell a thumb-footed marsupial that.
Dogs crave the pork bones they buried
in your lily rows. You planted them lilies
too close, the neighbor says. Is it blue
bags or paper tonight. She's set her evil eye
on the laid-off man who drops his dogshit
down the storm drains, noted the quivering
tails of his hounds, who stalked the zoo
wallaby down till they wore him out.
Those dogs live one block down and one
block over, yowl all day to heavy metal music.
Pour boiling H_2O in your weedcracks,
even gasoline. That's how we always do it.
Why waste good money on spray. Look how white
those McKenzie kids are, don't they ever get outside.
Fish fry grease will wilt that creeping nightshade,
curl it up like witch feet. Why would you tolerate
all that Creeping Charlie. But don't it smell fine
when it's mowed. Neighbors crave other neighbors
to pass their primordial insights to. God rest
the zoo wallaby, cornered by Laidoff's shelter saves,
dragging their clanking chain lightning around from one
to another place nobody wants them. How much
will they charge Laidoff for the wallaby
harassed and harangued to death while the he-wolves

and she-wolves howled in their enclosures.
What did the slow-pacing bobcat think
when he heard that death racket. Bet he craved
some of that wallaby action, hey, born
as he is to rip out throats. Only the possum
heard it all. Only he knows, and damned
if he's going to say. His roof is your car's
underbelly, his carpet your driveway gravel.
Breakfast is beetles and snails plus whatever
you threw out. Ditto for dinner and lunch.
When you wish him a happy Trash Night he makes a face.

Blue Lake Fantasy #4

It is not commonly understood why my love is so deadly.
—Richard Jackson, *"Do Not Duplicate This Key"*

By a blue lake in early summer, at some glad reunion of mutual friends,
I'll be sitting just off the tide line, ripe to be stumbled upon
like a beautiful shell, when something old and wild calls you toward me.

It will have been years since you last saw my face, twisted and stained
with hatred and hundred proof tears, but now I'll look lovely
and strong, with well-toned legs tanned just the right shade

leading down from the lacy hem of my dress, and just the right streams
of blonde in my blunt-cut hair. You'll squint through your glasses,
shake your head, polite but expecting the worst:

gin on my breath, or a loaded gun in my innocent sack of corn chips
and sesame buns, one bullet engraved with your name.
(I bet you still think you can boss my dreams around!)

And a yellow-eyed cat curled up cool and soft
in the birches above us, will be licking her paws and purring
her cues; and of course I'll pretend not to see you

at first, but then when I turn toward my name
in the curve of your voice, in your uplifted question mark,
you'll smile and I'll gaze, backlit by sunset gold,

just past your face, my flattened palm a visor stretched brow
to brow, and say *Well, hello . . !* and let it trail off to mean anything,
nothing at all. You won't have to ask how I am; how else

could I be, serene and tanned and toned with just the right twirls
of blonde in my blunt-cut hair, blown back by just the right breeze,
and gazing just past you, my flattened palm a visor,

the cat curled up in the branches above our heads, purring
Well, look who's here! And then from the lake, a shape that might be
a wavepoint or drifting log will bloom sudden arms

and a waving hand and there like a slick wet otter will come
my new darling-who-loves-me, out of the blue lake
that shines and waits just over this length of fence.

Lucinda's Voice

I'm rocking out back in the hammock under the red maple cracked
in two by last week's storm, its spooky branches roost to a family
of crows who drive the purple finches from the clothesline
with their mammalian bawling, their gaudy sorrow older than our own.

From the kitchen the singer's voice slides down its raspy ladder,
undiluted lust. Collapsing and inflating and collapsing. She'll never
end up with her right true love. That's the forever storm she will not
be saved from. The crows proclaim their ancient sooth:

can't rock in their lonely crow tree and tell them lies. Lucinda's
voice bobs, each note a green sail, a gauzy scarf pinned to the clothesline.
I wish I could tell her my story—street lamps fried, maple limbs
crashing onto the porch, gutters torn off in the throat of the storm,

one book of matches left in the drawer. Spoiled meat and broken window
panes. One little finch comes back to the clothesline, hungry and brave,
white cord gripped in her wee bird claws. When she tweets her mate down,
he flits from the broken gutter toward the maple, cheep-cheeping

along to Lucinda, her voice low and canny as the crows'. *You told me I*
was your queen You wanted to paint my picture Her voice a big empty bed
with satin pillows. Since the night of the storm I've slept downstairs alone
on the star block quilt. For three days we broke maple branches, barely

speaking, stuffed our broken tree in forty bags. From cover of lilacs
the finches sparked for bugs. You and I don't even raise our
voices anymore. I wake when the crows warm up in their swindle song.
I slide out back and rock in the twigs and tall grass, awaiting your call.

A Smoke

By late afternoon on the coldest day of the year
he'd worked himself up to the highest peak,
stripping black shingles pitched to fall over the porch
in moldy patches as sky would soon fall,

Old Testament sky, shot with red arrows into starry
indigo. He'd cast off the safety line that bound
him to our house, new father who'd named
his new daughter after the white rapper's daughter,

young roofer with most at stake. And now
he was straddling the roof peak in silhouette,
tufty blonde hair gelled into chunks, square block
of jaw, a cigarette held in the vise of his lips.

He wanted the job done, wanted his money.
This morning he'd been the first to arrive in blue
darkness, below zero wind chill, in holey gloves,
a frayed scarf tied under violet rings of bruises

around his eyes, a jammed-on cap. Hopping side
to side lightly to warm himself along little rises
of snow in blue streetlight, he refused the thermos
of coffee until we insisted, reek trails of whiskey

when he exhaled, smoke of tobacco and frost
and fermented night. Imagine the lavender day-glo
nap on the backs of his daughter's toy ponies,
same color of snow melting out of his boot treads

onto the tavern floor. Maybe the ghost of his Purple
Heart uncle bought the first shot, or the ghost
of his grandfather killed by a falling log, or the father
gone out for cigarettes who lit down the tracks

to Idaho leaving one son to raise the rest. Maybe
they all shared a smoke on the roof last night,
from the same wrinkled pack, as you and your loves
and all of your dolls slept sweetly beneath new shingles.

II

Morning Swim

Which loneliness is finest? Confections of nights turned
apricot mornings, afternoon naps and rooms

wrapped in velvet, music pushing through birdshot
windows cracked by little boy guns, bang smashes of boys

pouring out of the woods and fields trailed by yellow sparks.
And if we do hunt the one thing we cannot kill, stumbling

on after its quickening heels, pulling up soft clods of earth
that is ours to ruin, what is the slowest, most roundabout way?

All of these years and ways I have loved you, bride to groom,
I've loved you best gone, away with your fires and cold ashes,

your fat and sated darlings, thirsty crew packed up and gone
from a kitchen full of empty cups and overlapping rings

on the counters and floors where they sat and sweated, full
or half full of the taste, the curious taste, the familiar, familial,

family taste. Past misplaced cars and mysterious bruises, I kick
and stroke and surrender my store of air. I've loved you best

alone, unwed, in rented beds or spread out on a stranger's grass
in the almost-light, the blur of the muted world, the world

under water, unreal startling blue of the pool's deep floor
or the blue-black currents of girlhood lakes, face down

in the water, over the slick weeds' tangle and muck, my strong
legs kicking away from you. Alive and kicking.

A Particular Shadow

A streetlight for one particular shadow,
a driveway for those two tracks. Everything
waits so hard. A doorway to fill with one shape.
Soup bones to bleed the last of their marrow,
sheets to be soiled and washed. And always
a lamp left burning, tiny whirr of filament.
A woman is smiling into her mirror and brushing
her hair again, preparing, adorning. The hurry
up and wait. And telephones, electricity
of wait. Empty rooms and empty chairs,
museums of waiting. A woman is marking pages,
then setting her book on the nightstand
and closing her eyes. She waits through bad
music, long meals, dull company. Into a frozen
boot print, a fresh fall of new snow on old,
that kind of wait, for a certain red jacket
to swing from a door hook. And after the leaving
finally begins, the next wait: *that* wait,
and then this. And now this.

And Woke Up Vanishing

Quick: name the seven sorrows,
the seven laments. Surely
they all have something to do
with vanishing—loggerhead, polar bear,
sea otter, middle class.
Out on some borderline
some mark of in between
I lay down golden in time
and woke up vanishing . . .
sang the beautiful blonde
with even more brain and soul
than cheekbone, and we sang
along with her into the fade.

Let's think of seven words for *vanish*
before we do, as the man on the radio
talks about time stratified:
When you reach a certain age,
he says, this afternoon's not just
this afternoon, but an afternoon
twenty-five years ago. Layers
of space and lines of occasion taper
into a wash, disintegrate.
There are people from twenty-five years ago
I wouldn't invite to my now.

Two stories, quick, before
we disintegrate. In one
there's a middle-aged woman
drinking a tall ginger mocha
with whipped cocoa-dusted cream.
And a posse of teenage girls
walks into the sunlit café,
their jaws aflame. Their jangly hair
makes an entrance of its own;
then one shrugs and says *shit, man,*
there's nobody here. Tell me
a word for bleached into the wall.

And then there's the man at the hotel
I saw pacing the horseshoe driveway,
rubbing his watchband and humming
a rash of mismatched notes.
His lover was late or maybe
not coming at all. From my place
on the terrace, I smelled his dread
rising out of my crème brulee.

As I scraped at the last streaks of
caramel, he turned on his heels
and headed into the woods,
hands in pockets, whistling. Tonight
was tonight and the twenty-five years
his outline's blurred into the treeline,
the woods' embrace. Are those

the man's outstretched arms or the long
limbs of birches? That raggedy catch
of breath in his lungs is the same
net of grief that felled the first of us.

Minnesota

That's my Middle West . . . the frosty dark.
—Nick Carraway, The Great Gatsby

Down here in late November geraniums wait out the killing frost,
brilliant in their last days. Afternoons like this we drank
at my kitchen table, laughing, crushing out smokes, beer
after beer, till the basement neighbors banged our loud music
down. Slap-happy young drunks in some kind of love, we waited
for the craziness to take us. You praised my reckless imagination

between visits to your girlfriend in the city, half-imagined
a life spent helping me down from barstools. On the prairie the frost
spread its pretty fans inside window panes. I'd never waited
so hard for a man, through such cruel cold. Alone with my drink
and True Menthols I graded papers, sang along to the music
of famous sad women, sank into love with lukewarm beer

and melancholy. I danced to the twist-tango head tease of beers-
in-progress, circling a comma splice here, a run-on there, imagining
you in the city drenched in citrus cologne and supper club music—
two of the broasted chicken, two ice waters, hold the frost—
while I dined on gas station burritos. Sundays all I'd get to drink
was 3.2, but I was brilliant in those last days, and you couldn't wait

to get back to me and tell me your big city tales, the thrilling weight
of your secret life concealed under lumberjack shirt and heavy beard.
In my town of 6,000 the men played cards, ate lutefisk and drank
while their women rosemaled homeland flora, rolled lefse, imagined
grandchildren as the bank clock blinked minus and engine blocks froze.
Why must confession go out of style just when I want to confess? Music

of our talk is what I craved more than drink or smoke, the exquisite music
or your voice tuned to mine. *You're my little oasis,* you said, and I waited
three days indoors to hear that; out on the highway a person could freeze
off fingers pumping gas. We made fake fire in the fake fireplace, hot beer-
flavored makeouts. I dreamt of a college exam on Fitzgerald (imagine!)
and woke saying, *It takes two to make an accident.* Drinking's

a life of parched lips and grave misreadings. A wracking cough, a drink
spattered onto a dance floor. I wonder how we are spared when I hear music
from those days, some wiry dinosaur swinging what's left of his ass, imagine
your wife and her tow-headed children crammed into a hippie van. Waiting
for cold and snow, for holdout flowers to give it up, how could I ever bear
to wish you good fortune? In your Minnesota, the plowed-under stalks freeze

to topsoil, waiting for wind to bear them into tassel, into bloom.
Who'd believe I'd give up drink, or the music of all-night talk
to be frozen into household, delivered out of wilderness to safety?
  Imagine.

I Remember How This Song Goes

When John comes back from the bar with another
big red drink, it might as well be the Del Rio, Ann Arbor,
circa '79, but no it's the Velvet Dog, New Orleans,
21st Century. Alcohol whispers where you been girl,

we missed you, welcome back. Josie asks who wants to play
the drinking game called "I Never." We've never
smoked angel dust or stolen a tip. Paula lays down
her last sin and says count me out. But I love the little gold

lights on the ceiling, and I'd love another big red
drink. I love those jangling guitars splashing out of the juke,
guitars of torn fingernails, rhinestone crowns.
And I love this song about galloping horses, soda-pop punk.

There is a storm in the form of a girl and a boy in a black-feather
boa's skateboarding away. He's left a half-pack of Newports
on the bar, and if I have another drink I'll be smoking again,
snap out of it snap but it's coming back and there's no

place like it. Breathe back the smoke of a hundred cigarettes
in the sparkly pink song of let's have another, quick, before
it all melts into smeared lashes neverland phone calls
odd bruises lost shoes and bare feet on broken glass.

Bottom of the Cup

Get used to it, says fortune man Otis Pepper,
tracing the webbing of lines in my palm
and stacking his deck to reveal a magician
charged with the power to transform my troubles
to charms. *Ain't never going to happen, hon.*
That'll be forty bucks.
But you a real lady, and smart,
you do just fine.
This fortune inspires a double shrimp
platter washed down with a Hurricane,
the better to dip you in deep-fried
voodoo, suck you down with sad tidings
from Otis Pepper, mystic sweetheart, love
doctor of no degrees. *Girl, you should count*
your angels. Try being gay and psychic
in bayou country! Happy New Year.
By spring I am used to the lack of you, except
to want to share this path of prairie
shorn into a maze, this June day sunny and cool,
fragrant with mowing. And tell you the names
of flowers I pass: spiderwort, yarrow, sparks of phlox.
Trill of a cardinal—no, I won't list the birdsongs.
Out back of town they've piled a season's
felled branches, ripe for ignition, inside a circle
of boulders. The whole village comes to watch.
What, after all of this time, have I ever required,

except requiring you? You without whom
I have so long burned and sung of burning.
July in high desert: hot, hot. Sad history of conquest,
sad-eyed dogs. Day-glo chrysanthemums left
for beloved dead in curls of highway. By now you should be
the tail of the Rio Grande, a trickle too low for rafting,
or a faded ristra strung on a flaking porch post.
   Here is the church of St. Francis, hunched
like an elephant into the Ranchos square. Inside its chambers
of mud and straw we genuflect and cross and strike
our breasts. Outside on a path of red dirt
there's a heifer's skull, her wormy jimson crown.
   And outside a Vermont window now, green mountain
of moose and owl. Spare you the names of trees,
the names of lakes, the shades of August; call it green.
This morning I climbed a hill so steep I could feel clumps
of muscles working, dividing, gathering.
The sky was a twirl-a-round heaven embellished
with blown-out clouds, the kind girls could carve
into horses, flank and mane. Swimming the nameless
lake, I knew my shoulders as my own, thought
these are my shoulders my trunk, my burning branches.
Out loud I said *sturdy,* if nothing else, I am sturdy.
That doesn't mean strong.

Room-Darkening Shades

When she comes back from burying
    her mother—no, the ashes

her mother's burned into—she comes
    with school photographs, cross-stitched linens,

ropes of fake pastel pearls and a genuine opal
    ringed with diamond chips inside a green

velvet box, wearing her mother's
    black coat and scarf, her mother's

pearl-cuffed party gloves. She isn't the first-ever
    woman to lose a mother, her husband

reminds her, watching her paint the bedroom walls
    cinnamon walnut, watching her hang the new shades,

square and solid, to keep the night inside. You're not
    the first-ever daughter to grieve, he says, yanking

the shades off the spool to the floor, letting the summer
    pinks through the lace at five a.m. when birds

begin to caw and scrap for seed. Nights when he sets
    the sleep machine to brook babble, light rattle path

through digital pebbles and reaches for her, she turns the dial
    back to the rumble and crash of waterfall into the well,

that sound she remembers from drinking herself down there,
    and even in the brightness of her garden, she recedes

into ferns or kneels in tall shoots of chestnut. Alone in the window,
    finally emptied of patience, he says *I loved her, too,*

she was my mother too, but his woman
    is already dressed for the will-have-been-gone, adorned

in her future's perfect black coat and scarf,
    and she's not the first ever to go.

Leaf by Leaf

(R.H., 1962–2001)

Let the slugs take the hollyhocks, trash
the dank saucers of beer where they lay down in threes
and gorged, drowning in honeyed surrender,
the garden gnawed into swags of green lace leaf by leaf,
slick-toothed destroyers crawling the highway veins.
Let the body do what it wants, the belly
round out to its perfect globe, the breasts tumble forth
from their elastic vault. A woman I know has hung herself
in a sunset-colored dress, each of her closing requests
a tiny planet. A week ago we shared a glass
of wine. Somebody folds her slender arms.
Somebody makes a cross and kisses his thumb.
Somebody else makes sure her silver earrings
get to Lucy, gold to Joan. Why not let the garden go
where it's always been going, down
in its wondrous excursion? *June bug vs. hurricane,*
and then the steady rain. Your Honor I hereby relinquish,
whatever's left in puddles then to vapor. Your Highness
I therefore yield. One of my tender rabbits to every stray.
To each of your blue-black crows, a shining eye.

III

What's Going On

Summer of nineteen seventy-something,
somebody's little sister has a baby.

We all drive the sixty miles of Metro artery
into Detroit's sooty heart to see for ourselves.

Blazing full-blown daylily summer, bulldozers
pulling up malls in the immigrant fields,

four or five long-haired girls in a Mustang,
windows down and wailing to Marvin Gaye

you know we've got to find a way
to bring some loving here today

One of us now an aunt with a big stuffed dog
in a carful of big stuffed hungover

heads with freshly shampooed bangs.
All of our fathers are drinking men

father, father everybody thinks we're wrong

and all of our mothers are lousy cooks. All of us girls
wear pink lip gloss and smoke Kool Kings.

Whose father makes the basement wine,
the clear corn liquor we siphon and sweeten

with 7UP and cherries? Whose mother
makes the borscht and bitter cabbage rolls?

Whose father knocks whose mother
down the stairs? Whose father gets

laid off and lets the lawn grow back to prairie?
Whose mother hangs the Christ heart

stuck with thorns on the kitchen wall
above the stove? Take this and eat

and spiders hatch in vacuum cleaner bags.
And we lift the new child up

in the swaddling light
of Henry Ford General Motors where

his mother will spend the bright coins
of her teens her twenties her thirties her forties

mother, mother, mother there's far too many
of you crying

Somebody's mother says girls get that straggly
hair out of your face, hold up your heads.

My Brother Calls Me from His Boat

Ship to shore: behind his faint voice the buck
and rock of lake waves slapping fiberglass, sultry
August night. On his new girlfriend's cell.
She's a dental hygiene student named Dupree,
twenty years younger, flossing him for practice.
I got the cleanest white smile these days, my brother says,
in the lilt that betrays his tipsiness, forecasts the first almost-innocent
snippet of cruelty one hair's breadth over the rim of charm.
My brother sets up his camp on that rim, dances its giddy
width in steel-toed boots while the rest of us watch
spellbound, afraid he'll fall again, afraid he won't.

When we were children, my brother and I learned to ski
across the glittering lakes of upper Michigan.
The uncles took turns on the boat between beers
while our steely fins cut through the water lilies.
Meanwhile the dozen sentry aunts on shore cupped hands
over eyes and squinted as they marked us,
shrieked when our lifejackets came untied,
hooted when we dropped a ski. Here's where you'd want
to know if my brother skied barefoot or blew up frogs.
Here's about when he should start to tip wrong:
the touch of a wayward priest or a call to the napalm jungle,
tattoo curse of a bayoneted heart. But my brother ate hot dogs
and peed in the woods like the rest of us kids
in wet bathing suits, a boy merely beloved, called inside

for pie and ice cream, the flag of his Mickey Mouse
beach towel waving dry in pine-drenched breeze.

And now my brother calls me from his boat, shitfaced
to shore, and he sounds so lonely you might forgive
the smashed cars, the threats that sent boyfriends sprinting,
the dozens of powder blue rosaries said for nothing.
Why don't you swim over, he says, *and have a drink.*
That is . . . if you're not too good for us . . . college girl.
When I close my eyes: the light smacking sound of lake
and the rainbowed gasoline, circling my brother's boat.

My Father's Drums

His mad jazz slammed its way up basement stairs
through closed doors and double-glazed windows
all over the neighborhood. *The one true
American art form,* he called it, records turned up so loud
the floorboards buzzed. No rock and roll
allowed. No three-chord progressions in this house;
no rudimentary hook, no bridge, no lame refrain,
no silly haircuts please, we are *musicians.*
Bashing along with the hi-fi he banged through our days and nights
with a rat-a-tat rage, the fury fired down from his shoulders,
shot into his wrists. When he pounded his high-hats,
the pictures flew off their nails. *Woodchopper's Ball;
The Big Crash from China; Sing, Sing, Sing;
Mercy, Mercy, Mercy.* Never the whiz of his belt buckle,
never the sting of his open hand, only those long incredulous looks
whenever we smarted off, when his head came around
in slow motion, eyes narrowed, lips curling into a deep
underwater snarl: *What did you say to me, Mister?
Young lady, what-did-you-just-say-to-me?*
Sometimes we thought he beat them instead,
rattled their cymbals and snares to spare the dullard
child brains inside our skulls, wore down
their tight-stretched skins with his hammering sticks
to save our lackluster souls, our sorry hides.

The Man Who Says Pain Is a Friend

The old man will never hire help, insists
on mowing the whole bloody acre himself,
but lets us all pay for it later as he rehydrates
with Pabst Blue Ribbon, curses the August
heat and the pretzel salt he's not allowed,
takes off his glasses to swipe the slippery bridge
of his nose, curses his shooting-star muscle pains
up, down and sideways, his thundering joints
as he flips the recliner back, curses the t.v. guide,
goddamn it all. The man who says pain is a friend
is no friend of mine. By God, how I'd love to give
him some, days when my father's body seems strung
with glass and his spine crackles into shards, shoulders
and hips shot with random slivers, kneecaps full of marbles.
His own father died in pine shade, planting roses
in front of his cedar log hunting camp, the Escanaba still
when his arm buzzed electric, his heart misfired.
Let's say he was conjuring deer and woodsmoke
when he went, one hand on his heart, his eyes set
upon the green river, reflective of nothing like pain.

Drinking Man

Out on the edge of the highway, under the mailbox,
the mourning dove is hobbling, something important broken.

Through the kitchen window, my father sees three boys
poking at her with sticks, slams his cup on the counter,

runs with his fury down the drive *stop it goddamn you
sick punks should be ashamed, sick punks,*

scoops the dove into the cradle of his big hands, speaks
comfort to her in coo-tones, carries her out to the back

and lays her tenderly on the lawn *Jesus Christ almighty.*
Digs around for a sharp enough rock. Mom and I

stand at the window *leave him alone* as he raises his arm
twice and can't bring it down, then on the third try

crushes the dove's toy skull *don't say anything to him,* comes in
to wash his hands, and drinks his coffee. *Nature doesn't care,*

he finally mutters. Mom and I throw in a load
of whites, hang out a load of colors. She pinches the back of my neck

with a clothespin, says *The next time you think
your old man is a bastard, better remember this morning.*

Oh Honey

Her chest is a railroad, honey-greased
tracks, sure engine of heartbeat pumping
heads of steam. On the white cloth,

I lather the soap, dab the incisions,
rinse the white cloth, then dab and rinse
again. I declare her shoulders mine

entirely, claim the twin curves
of my mother's solid rump,
her folds and caves, plump stomach,

spill of breasts, sure muscles dividing
into her slender calves, her fine-boned
wrists. Because I am cut from her body

the seep of my mother's wounds
does not offend me. Long bend
of river carved into her leg, oozing

the thick sliding color of honey,
a sweetness called out from the core
of my mother, river of gold

and it's all I can do not to kneel and stare,
built as I am from her river of milk.

Because I was pulled

through a slit in her belly,
I bend down to bandage my mother
clumsy with gratitude,

her chest split from neck to navel,
her leg split from ankle to crotch.
My mother squeezes the honey paste

onto my fingertips, unwinds
the roll of gauze. Oh honey, she tells me,
what a good job you're doing.

Felonious

Cousin Jerry's felonious now.
In the newspaper photo this morning
his famous grin's composed
of pencil-point dots, still freckled
forty year-old imp on his way upstate
for robbery, armed and dangerous.
   Remember him hanging
by knees and wits from the top bunk
at grandfather's cabin, blue darts of eyes crossed,
tongue red from cinnamon hearts
stuck out and wagging. *Girly-boobs, girly-boobs,*
look who's got her girly-boobs! Jerry's
   a bona fide criminal now, forget
the firecrackers and window wax; forget
how he'd splash all us little ones, hold
our heads underwater till bubbles swirled.
He made us eat poison berries, then peed his own pants
when bears came down to drink.
   Remember he bought that dime-store
Beatles love song, begged and then threatened
before we gave in to his tight-lipped kiss,
then sucked his dirty thumb white when he thought
we were asleep. *I've known the secret*
for a week or two. Nobody knows, just we two. Oh Jerry
why can't you be good.
   Look how he flips the bird

for all the wide world to see as the lawman palms
the arc of Jerry's skull and dunks him
into the squad's back seat, slams
his big door on the nasty boy for whom
one girl would do as well as any, the Jerry
who jimmied pink vinyl diary locks,
read pages aloud to the uncles. The Jerry
who stole lavender sachets
stashed in panties drawers. *Listen.*
  Do you want to know a secret?
Do you promise not to tell? Oh Jerry
come closer, Jerry stay gone, Jerry
come back so that I can resist or open
my mouth and kiss you, really kiss you.

Tiger

This afternoon as I watch him through the shutter slats,
rolling in crackling red chestnut leaves, tied out
on the long leash attached to his jingle bell collar,
I finally say out loud he's getting smaller.

I watch from inside, where it's warm, little stack
of papers on my lap, mug of sweet blond coffee.
He's a rangy young tomcat, cancer of the liver,
outlook wicked. Vet gave us three doses of prednisone

six months ago, looked down at his notes and told us
he was sorry. Toby's gone through six refills now,
one hundred and eighty-seven lucky doses. Each morning
one of us pries his cat hinges open, jabs down his throat

a tiny white disk of steroid, white stone in the gears
of his death clock. We swallow it with him
the way we have swallowed our prayers for a world gone
to hell in a basket, as predicted by our fathers

and their fathers. The perfect Wisconsin boys
still shove off to war from Green Bay, as my uncle did
sixty years ago, wavy black hair shaved and swept away,
belly hard with purpose. *Father, I'm scared,* he said

to the priest on dock duty, and the priest said, Son,
get your ass on that boat. Toby pees hard
on the withering ivy, sprays the cedar fence.
I forgive him the baby sparrow, the chipmunk, the smelly

business in the ferns. He stretches his rickety
length and rolls, unlocks the pink of his mouth
and talks his cat talk to the grass, to the sky—
the tiger he came from, the tiger he's going to.

Eastertide 2003

The Lord is about to lay down His purple voodoo
on a rainy day shot with guilt and chocolate eggs.

Cat should have died six months ago.
He stretches his razored bones in the sunlit weeds.

A laid-off couple wanders the aisles of Target,
wondering how they'll afford the ninety dollars.

The woman blowing her nose in the therapist's chair
imagines the pints of Cherry Garcia melting in her trunk.

As the president mispronounces another important word,
the old women count their moles and tighten their shawls.

So that the evil bishops can't intercede, the virgin appears,
but to dim-witted folk who mistake her for Pyrenees fairies.

The general reminds us that looting is fun and natural
for the oppressed. Good news for American window glass.

When the priest sashays toward us, shaking a branch of holy-dipt pine,
we rock back in our pews to absorb the liqueur of saints.

St. Catherine lived for years on pus and communion wafers.
We come home to jello, ham, and pink bunny cake.

While cousin Siobahn channels the Celtic ancestors,
we grow nostalgic for days when she snorted coke.

Fear not, for we are your liberators. Which way
to your gold and frankincense and myrrh?

Anything that can happen is happening somewhere near.
The stone rolls away to reveal a Jeep Liberty

as the Bachelorette makes her excruciating choice
and the soldier's boot displaces the first grain of sand.

Covet

for Jan

A dollar thirty-nine at Denny's Sure-Fine: sprays of peach glads unwrapping
in tall cans, bright among aisles of soap and tortillas. I want
these flowers so much I would steal them, as much as my mother wanted
that 12¢ bottle of *Deep Sea Coral Pink*, a discontinued color in the winter

of 1957. Not postage stamps, not the library cookbook *Exciting Ways with
Ground Meats*, but nail polish, something beautiful for her hands. I want
to make lunch of these flowers, drink in their color. My mother had rolled
the bottle into her palm, was just about to pocket it. Imagine the boss

of S.S. Kresge looking down from his father's desk in the managerial loft
at that rare moment when my mother had chosen sin, and alerting cosmetic
personnel—STOP, THIEF!—or worse the stern tenderness (*ma'am, were you
meaning to pay for that polish, that's twelve cents plus the tax.*)

Hushed call to my father, soft slide of confessional screen. And then the
benevolent *go in peace, and covet no longer the things of this world, such as
pointy pink nails* . . . Perhaps her case thinly disguised in next Sunday's sermon:
young mothers who yearn too wildly for worldly pink things. O pray us up

from our longing, we who so love the fragrance and skin
of the merchandise of Earth. Whose flesh is the flesh of the iPod,

the fair trade Sumatra, the Whole Foods olive bar. Clinique's bonus bag.

And buckets of coral blooms in every Sure-Fine. World without end, amen.

IV

That Teenage Feeling

O sainted girls, divine Mademoiselles,
help me make sense of your tedious
adoration—two thousand years of incense
smoke and fingerbones wound with rubies,
souring sponges and slop pails, stiff-wired
brushes better to shred young knuckleskin.

What grace makes its home in the robin's
egg folds of your star-sprinkled gowns?
What should we glean from your orgasmic
smiles, and how does it feel to wrap
His ring with pink angora for your chain,
feel it bounce lightly between your breasts?

Nights in your cell, upon your stony pallet,
you long so *exactly*—such exquisite longing!
Stuck in vague fits of desire the rest of us pray
for a groom like yours, whose flesh is mountain,
ocean, sky. A wafer of light in your open throat,
and his born-ancient body melts upon your tongue;
swallow and you are holy, wholly His.

Under your habit, the goat hairs prickle,
and nettle wreaths punish your thinning
wrists. *Dear Diary, he came to my cell
with a corsage of charred forget-me-nots.*

*He said without words that I should not be long
within these walls.* My building has many units, spake
the Lord. A lifelong lease gets you a mat, a hunk
of daily bread. The martyrs shall spin you a tunic
the moths have embroidered with tiny holes.

*Diary, every other boy's too safe and much
too sensible.* Wouldn't any girl burn
her plans to watch her worldly husk float
over the back yard barbeque, shed
for wings? Who wouldn't starve for a halo
of homecoming crowns or scale the walls
of hell to win His Class of Infinity ring?

Ravenous

I ate a whole honeydew this way once,
when Kenny and I broke up,
standing just like this in my nightgown
at the kitchen sink, with the wrong
kind of knife, slicing overripe pastel wedges
from stony rind thinking *pieces of moon*
because I was stoned, rocking the blade
back and forth, my elbows cold with juice,
my chin jutting out as I used bottom teeth to scrape
off the last grooves of fruit. This time it's last night's
crab legs between my jaws, a nutcracker
in the drawer but I will not stop; I want
to use fangs to crack the shells, then all
ten fingers to rip and disjoint and pull,
so let me work. Midnight in the kitchen, sink lit
by a buzzing blue tube, I don't have to look up
to the window to see who I am: a wild-haired
cartoon girl astonished by her hunger.
The sink fills with craggy pink moonscapes,
empty claws, their sucked-out flesh
fishy-sweet in my mouth as I bite and chew
and swallow, make a fist to wipe my chin.

Desire

I'm not where I should be, washing a load of whites
or correcting papers. All else before you is small,
desire, sweet emergency, don't ask me where
we are or what we're doing. Crisis in your eyes,
and in your hands—I can't bear to remember
your hands; I could eat them, each finger
a meal in itself. Won't dare to imagine your neck,
nor its prickly man-scented, squared-off hairline; better
the sudsy load of sweat socks and towels, it's/its errors,
In today's society transitions. You and I step
through these dream gates together, each swinging door
a monstrous, ornate D. Town without pity, city of sinner-saints,
city that never sleeps. Open all night and Christmas and oh,
let go my hand; no, take it, take them both—
I can't bear my empty hands, my empty
throat, my little town, my bed empty of you.

Newlywed

I stumbled into furniture, terry robe reeking
of garlic and fabric softener, wiping
my new husband's whisker-hairs off the sink
each morning, mourning the little moons
of his toenail clippings. I took stacks of cookbooks
out on the dock, read recipes to the mallards. Each night
was a gourmet feast my new husband doused with ketchup
as the walls of the old world were falling on CNN.
And then he'd retire to his study to tenure himself.
    When the Maytag broke down I shuddered
with hope and joy. The calendar told me 1991,
but I wanted to crawl back into Khrushchev's big lap.
Now I was married—what was there left to fear?
The Soviet Union is over, I said to the Maytag repairman,
but his head was inside the agitator tub.
Russia is over, I told the back of his coveralls,
and they answered he didn't care for politics.
    On our first anniversary I'd gone out to re-check the mail,
and behold, the Stealth Bomber's monster shadow
fell over the driveway. Imagine its silent approach
and its trailing horrors. Imagine my leaping heart.
Which corner of the basement had my father stashed
the kidney beans and jam in '62? Where
was the nearest atomic-proof shopping center?
    It's only the airplane convention, my neighbor
assured as the Concorde buzzed our hairdos.

She was learning courtroom stenography
because her husband was always off hunting.
He needs to find something to shoot at or hook,
she confided, *or he can't be happy.*
He'd follow the caribou around like they were the Grateful Dead.
She was too young to remember Nikita's curse,
his pounding shoe, but I made stroganoff for lunch.
We drank cappuccino from her new machine
while the river beyond us rose and fell,
our husbands off hunting whatever was left to hunt.

Faculty Wife with Hummus

Charmed, I'm sure, to meet you. I made
the hummus—marbled blue pottery bowl
just south of the shrimp, and topped with cilantro,

and I made the bowl. Never mind that I spent today
trotting my Birkies all over your town in search
of tahini. *Tahini*—it's sesame paste, ground up

sesame seeds; one teaspoon can add three pounds.
Hummus is that, and garlic and mashed chick
peas—garbanzo beans—I soaked them

raw and hard all night while my husband
hacked into another grant proposal. Thanks,
it's a raku glaze, and try the hummus.

I had a job where they used to call me *Ms.*
I was in charge of a staff of twenty-five.
I have a double masters in Yin and Yang.

Please try my hummus, a Middle Eastern
staple, a sesame-bean pâté. Four stores
for a raggedy bunch of cilantro. Four languages

I speak fluently: French, Russian, Greek,
and Portuguese. Where in this town can I go
for fresh portobellos? Is there an artichoke

east of Elk Mound? How do you cope
with six months of ice and snow?
Where is the nearest place I can climb some rocks?

Can I wrap you some hummus to go?
I had a job with a parking space reserved.
Pantyhose and lipstick every day.

Soaked overnight, not canned.
Four cloves of garlic peeled
and pestled fresh, by my own hand.

The Goat

From day one the goat despised me. Apparent
in her backward lunge, her horizontal scrutiny.
The rooster, cat, and dog merely indifferent,
all slurping from the same enormous bowl;

the mother just north of aloof. *You are a bit
too glamorous for my son,* she often said.
Lipstick hater, mascara hater, brewer of foul-
smelling teas. And the curse of the cabin, itself

an organic, growing thing, drafts stuffed with dirty straw.
No one dared mention why it was worth
the goat's feed and wrath when cheese was as natural
and local down the street at the Red Owl store.

No one asked what were the little black flecks
in the honeycomb where bees' legs stuck,
why the homemade wheat pasta quivered, glutinous,
under the wormy tomatoes. And nobody switched the station

from NPR, not even when folkies screeched whaling songs,
so powerful was the charm of a non-smoking man
who could cook and grow herbs and build cabins
and love his mother. Could make his own ice cream,

croon in Norwegian to ancient wives as he led them
gently around on the VFW dancefloor, princely in
coveralls. No wonder I was hollow-eyed starved
when you found me, your promise of vodka and cheetos

and rock and roll! How willingly I leapt into your leather
seats, inhaled the bouquet of smoke and air conditioning.
How delighted those nights you surprised me with Mrs. Paul's
and tater tots, baked at 350 upon our return from Best Western's

Happy Hour. Battered and golden, abundant with greases
and salts! How grateful I was to be even your second
choice, slopping that feast with ketchup and tartar,
forgiving the tiny crystals of ice at the core of each scalding bite.

Panic in Detroit

The first balmy night of April, magnolia buds aimed to fire into May,
I ask *please let's walk.* Only around the park trail, maybe a mile.
I want to lean in to your shoulder, your jacket's soft collar, make

the one tilted shadow we make. I don't want to be lonely the way
I've been, crying into the sink. And so I walk, a woman alone
in the park at night, and sing above apprehension this song

from the seventies. The lyrics don't ever make sense but they feel
good, called out from the cave of my chest, the college girl code
for everything gone to hell or heaven-bound: *Panic in Detroit,*

so don't wait up! I wrote those words to my roommates
in a notebook we left by the phone, my happy scrawl three
sheets deep, the night Sam took me downtown for my first blues,

a night like this thirty years ago, *sweet daddy let me follow you down.*
The club doors stayed open; a soft city wind hummed the bass line,
hauling the blue smoke, blue notes over the Detroit River.

By the time we got back to Sam's, the sun had pressed magnolia
into bullets, all over his back yard. We pulled a few twigs for vases.
By noon they would open fire on the house, petal shrapnel, pink lead,

artillery of heaven. Gritty from blues, smoke rising out of our hair,
we lay down on the slick wood floor and slept through the afternoon,
the way you and I would sleep after panic of making love—a hard,

animal sleep brought on by crushed blossom potion dripped
into drowsy eyes. One wakes from such sleep in love with the first thing
she sees, be it man or beast or curls of magnolia wilting in her hands.

Still Enough

Standing dumbstruck still
in this neck-tall grass
when the doe blinks once,

then bends her head,
then goes wherever she goes,
and then I am nobody

you would know, a roundness
blurred into buttercups,
coneflowers, blazing star,

floating this waving lake
of flowering grasses,
in almost over my head

till the deerfly finds me, stings
just below an ear.
So what if I disappeared

out here, lay down
till the hide wore away
and the cage of ribs

held moonlit snow,
lay down till the hair
flew off in birdbeaks

and the skull bloomed
stars of moss?
If you're willing

to stand still enough
to be stung, you'll see
some astonishing things.

Raspberries

First the blue bay, then poplar ridge, flat
stubbled field, and dune spiked with deep-rooted
grass, the lush layer of clover
and milkweed clear to the road
and somewhere in there, in the thick
things, the ready berries sliding
from their stems to pickers'
coffee cans, lining the sides
with scarlet velveteen. And the boys
picking recklessly, creaming the bushes
ahead and hooting their bites and scratches
while one girl turns berries inside out
before setting each sweet rough
nap upon her tongue. And each one
tells the story of them all, each single orb
of glossy stain a continent, hard seed
to white flower to green thorn.

I'd bring you here if you were the following kind,
not disappeared deep into some sour patch of business.
This morning another husband
plods down a sand hill to sit on his fender
and smoke while his wife pulls handfuls of sweet
wild fruit she'll mash and freeze
and thicken with sugar, tuck
into the same luscious crust

her mother learned. Some Sunday
in winter they'll have this day back,
with cream. Or maybe they won't
be speaking by then; maybe it's all just
hungry speculation. Maybe the husband hates raspberries—
those infinitesimal hairs, pesky seeds stuck
in his molars. Maybe it's just
her own story she'll make, a trip to the market
for shortening and lemon, a kettle of tea, her kitchen's
sweet-sour smell as she rinses the crimson
stain from her nails, looks out
through open blinds. The one red bird,
sparrows clumped under the feeders.
Last leaves of maple surrendering
to layers of snow.

This Is Not My Beautiful House

I knew a man once who dared me to take off my clothes and run
down a rock jetty into the Atlantic. Dark on the beach and the bars
had all closed, a few slow cars cruising A1A, a few lone morning stars.
While I was swimming the man took my watch—a lucite-bubbled
thing from the 70s, ocean blue face—and smashed it with his boot.
He called himself a *natural man,* hated eyepaints and underwire bras,
my silver platform shoes. I wish he could see me now, my sun-ruined
skin shining with night cream, breasts unbound and slack under flannel,
cat and I half asleep on pillows in front of the fireplace, our shadows
leapfrogging the ceiling. The cat can't get near enough, her rump
pressed against the firescreen, pulling pawfuls of flannel from my hip,
nursing her life-deep dream.

The man once told me his love for high places could kill us. *If I look down
too long, I'll have to jump,* he'd say whenever we'd walk a bridge,
a*nd I'll take you with me.* Something in the water's song, tunnel spouts
calling his name. I hear his name and a hundred more whispered
down the chimney flue, outside a new frost upon old snow stuck
with debris, a few drops of rocky oil at its core. Tonight on the news
they warn about seeding clouds, wiring the wartime sky electric, concocting
a storm to turn back the enemy. They warn about hologram warplanes,
laser-cut fog. When he made love, the natural man would worry. He didn't
want children, hated their clutter more than the mess of spermicides.
I wonder where he wound up, with his hand-tooled time-smashing boots
and his terrible urges.

Sometimes now, walking, if I let myself sink into footsteps, I can't
tell where I am. Then, in a moment of panic or joy I remember the lake
is a lake, not an ocean, the woman is not who the girl used to be. Now
there's a house and it's waiting to be walked to. Take a left here and see
the red roof. Now I'm a wife who hangs lace in her kitchen
windows, the blue and green flags of her husband's shirts
on a tightrope behind the house. Now we're another creature.
The husband and his wife eat, go on vacation. And when they come
home it's the same as it ever was: the man builds a fire and the woman cooks,
and when the man climbs the stairs to his study, the woman arranges pillows
and quilts by the fireside, remembering the whirling storms, the chorus
of names she summoned, taking the dare.

At Ragdale

Once I asked myself, when was I happy?
I was looking at a February sky.
When did the light hold me and I didn't struggle?
                    —Deborah Digges, "Broom"

One morning in summer I lay—red ball tip
of a pushpin, tiny rise of texture, blip
on the screen of the world—under two hundred
years of elm, on a moth-gnawed
blanket dragged down a wooded path,
and slept in open air, with my books
and my apples and cheese and all good
intentions. Overhead in the branches,
black squirrels shook their tails
and chitted their complaints; black
crows cocked their satin heads,
while behind me a garden shot purple
with hollyhocks opened to prairie
splashed with orange with lilies.
Beyond that prairie a river poured cool
and a fox flicked her bright tail and drank,
and beyond her the city of Chicago cast
its great shadow over my parents' yellow house,
my mother bent over her crossword books, my father
with his bowl of peanuts, his long yellow
pads lined with history, and beyond them
my husband, feeding his cats and kissing

his ten thousand worries hello. And when
the sunlight passed itself down limb to limb,
and found me there dozing, I did not roll
out of the light or cover my eyes.

Junction

This morning, driving south from home, you saw
the land still waiting, hills of it piled up
around the barns in weary winter-rusted golds.
The road unwound to print the circling redtail,
splayed-out clouds, fallen hulls
of crib-caged corn, a sudden dark
roundness of tree trunks against flat sky.

What is it that you want *now*,
you asked yourself. A willow leans her yellow
leaves just inches from the surface of the water.
Whole eras pass by like road signs,
flash metallic, netted fish.
Slow curve, detour, right turn does not stop.
No breakdown lane, no now-or-never junction.

Meanwhile in this same sky, the great hinged
bellies of warplanes swing open and the headmistress
counts her children. And Icarus falls and falls
through every painting, all of our lives in line
like these little white crosses along the road.

What you want now: a county road that snakes
its crooked way up grey half-hills, down
the long rusty slopes, finds clusters of cows
and herds of deer at dusk,

blue chicory in ditches, green corn,
and the deep hush of amber before stars.

And you want them the way
you once wanted a drink, another
drink, a cigarette. The way you once wanted
his love, or *his* love, or *his*. But more. More.